# THE MONTREAL MUSEUM
# OF FINE ARTS

P9-AOM-175

POCKET GUIDE

This *Pocket Guide* has been published with funds provided by the Montreal Museum of Fine Arts' Volunteer Committee.

Texts and research: Hélène Lamarche
Photography of works:
    MMFA Photographic Services
Supervision: John Porter, Chief Curator
        Danielle Sauvage, Director of
        Communications

A production of the Publications Service
Co-ordination: Denise L. Bissonnette
Translation: Jo-Anne Hadley
Revision: Donald Pistolesi
Graphic design: Dallaire & Giguère Inc.
Electronic publishing: Macadam Inc.
Photo-engraving and printing: Litho Acme Inc.

Cover:
William Bouguereau, *Crown of Flowers* (detail),
no. 40

Legal deposit, 4th trimester 1991
Bibliothèque nationale du Québec
National Library of Canada
ISBN 2-89192-144-5

The Montreal Museum of Fine Arts
P.O. Box 3000, Station "H"
Montreal, Quebec, Canada
H3G 2T9

Printed in Canada

# Preface

The publication of this *Pocket Guide* to the Museum coincides with a turning point in the history of an institution that is over one hundred and thirty years old: the opening of a new pavilion and underground galleries linking it to the original building. The Galleries of Ancient Cultures connect the Jean-Noël Desmarais Pavilion, on the south side of Sherbrooke Street, to the Benaiah Gibb Pavilion on the north. The Museum can now display works of art that, for lack of gallery space, had been confined to the dark recesses of the reserves much too long.

For those who would like to have a quick glimpse of the richness and diversity of the Museum's collections, the *Pocket Guide* provides a selection of the most significant works. Chief Curator John R. Porter and his team of curators had the very difficult task of choosing sixty works from a collection that comprises over twenty-five thousand items. The accompanying texts were written by Hélène Lamarche, Head of the Educational and Cultural Service; and the Publications staff  was responsible for the *Guide*'s production.

It is with great pleasure that we invite all our visitors to wander through the Museum's galleries to discover the wonderful treasures they contain.

Pierre Théberge
Director

# Contents

# Foreword

Paul-Émile Borduas wrote that there are a thousand and one ways to experience a work of art. There are also a thousand and one ways to visit a museum. Using formal parallels drawn from art history or specific themes, the Museum suggests the first way when it organizes exhibitions and selects works from its collections for display. Each visitor uses the thousand others in his own way, ultimately choosing the way that suits him best.

This guide introduces the visitor to some sixty works of the Museum's collection by providing points of reference. There are no gallery by gallery descriptions, but rather an overview of the collection as a whole. Although the selection was made from the collection's major works, it is possible that at times not all of them will be on display. The Museum's commitments, such as loans to other institutions, and the ongoing task of restoration may sometimes require the installation of the galleries to be altered. Textiles and works on paper or wood can only be displayed for short periods of time because of their fragility and their sensitivity to light. As far as possible, the Information Desk receptionists will be pleased to keep visitors informed regarding these changes.

Works are generally grouped according to era, country or genre, and occasionally theme.

H.L.

# A Short History

The Montreal Museum of Fine Arts was established over a hundred and twenty-five years ago. It came into existence because of the desire of a group of Montrealers to provide Montreal with cultural institutions worthy of a flourishing North American city. Among the founders of the Art Association of Montreal in 1860 were businessmen such as Treasurer William H.A. Davies, Secretary Thomas Davies King and Councillor Benaiah Gibb; judges such as Charles Dewey Day and John Samuel McCord; and academics such as Thomas Sterry Hunt and Canon William Turnbull Leach, Dean of the Faculty of Arts at McGill College (later McGill University). The most active among the members was without doubt Lord Bishop Francis Fulford, Montreal's first Anglican bishop. All were of English or Scottish descent, except for the painter Napoléon Bourassa, who was the only French-Canadian member of the AAM for many years.

By the terms of the act of incorporation (April 23, 1860), the Association defined its mandate as follows:
For the encouragement of the Fine Arts, by means of the establishment and maintenance, in so far as may be found practicable of a Gallery or Galleries of Art . . .
The Association's immediate goals were to organize and present art exhibitions and lectures, and establish a library and a reading room devoted to art publications. Their long-range goals included the building of permanent premises. This project had to wait until 1879, when the bequest of Benaiah Gibb, one of the Association's founding members, permitted the Association to erect the first Canadian building specially designed to house collections of art.

This building, no longer standing, was located on the east side of Phillips Square, just steps away from Saint Catherine Street.

Less than ten years later, the Association reached its goals. In 1893, the building had to be expanded to accommodate the major collection of paintings donated by John W. Tempest. The turn of the century was a golden age for Montreal collectors, which included such eminent businessmen as Sir William Van Horne, Sir George A. Drummond, William John Learmont and Lord Strathcona.

Meanwhile, Montreal grew and changed: the tranquil Phillips Square of the 1880s was now at the very heart of the city's retail industry and the buildings that had grown up around the Museum obstructed the natural lighting needed for the art studios. When the time came to renovate, the Councillors no longer hesitated to recommend seeking a new location. The AAM installed itself permanently on Sherbrooke Street West in 1912 in a building designed by Montreal architects Edward & W.S. Maxwell. The Association's new home was expanded on two occasions, in 1939 and again in 1976, until the construction of the new pavilion by Moshe Safdie came to join the original building in 1991. The institution's name was changed from the Art Association of Montreal to the Montreal Museum of Fine Arts at the end of 1948.

# The Museum's Collection

Established in 1879 through a bequest from Benaiah Gibb, the Museum's collection has continued to expand and diversify. To the initial collection of paintings by European masters were added works of decorative art, prints and drawings, photographs and outstanding examples of contemporary art. Although the Permanent Collection encompasses a vast array of eras and countries, the Museum's collection of Canadian art is truly one of our most outstanding collections.

The collection of Canadian art comprises much more than a variety of forms of artistic creation: it reveals the evolution of Montreal society. Because the Association's founding members were influenced by Protestant tradition, they preferred portraits, landscapes, historical, literary and genre scenes to scenes of a religious nature. The pictorial art they selected – most often canvases of a type known as "easel painting" – was designed to be admired in the intimacy of the home, or at the very least in semi-private rooms, such as the galleries of Art Association's first building, whose ambience was reminiscent of Victorian drawing rooms.

For many Montrealers of French origin, art expressed a collective intention that was conveyed through the construction and ornamentation of churches and the erection of monuments and sculptures in parks and other public areas. Added to these differences was an attitude of reciprocal mistrust and reticence that had its roots in political events of the 19th century. In spite of Napoléon Bourassa's efforts, the realm of the visual arts also bore the stamp of Montreal's two solitudes.

Despite these dissimilarities, many young francophone artists, in particular Clarence Gagnon and Suzor-Coté, studied at the Association's school – the city's only art school until the opening of the École des Beaux-Arts de Montréal in 1922. Works by artists trained at the Association's school were among some of the first Canadian works to be acquired. Over the years, collectors and art lovers such as Jessie Dow, Dr. F.J. Shepherd, Robert Lindsay, and later the Bronfman and DeSèvre foundations encouraged talented Canadian artists by awarding scholarships and instituting acquisition funds for Canadian works. A. Sidney Dawes and various members of the Morrice family were also major contributors to the Museum's collection of Canadian art.

In 1916, F. Cleveland Morgan's donation established the Museum's collection of decorative arts. His generosity inspired other art lovers to contribute to the collection: Harry A. Norton (Roman glass), Lucile Pillow (British porcelain), David W. Parker and F. Cleveland Morgan (textiles) and Eleanore Morrice (glassware, stoneware and furniture). In 1922, Mabel Molson, recognizing the quality of early Quebec decorative arts, made the first of many generous donations towards the establishment of this collection.

It goes beyond the scope of this guide to give a complete history documenting all those who have contributed to making this one of Canada's leading museums. However, it is hoped that this glimpse of the Museum's early days gives the reader some insight into the generosity and dedication of Montreal's first patrons of the arts. Succeeding generations, committed to enhancing the collections begun by the Art Association's founders, have taken up the torch.

# Choice of Circuits

## Let's start in the middle...
### Galleries of Ancient Cultures

The Museum's collections are divided between the north (1912) and south (1991) pavilions, which are connected by a large underground gallery housing art from the Far East, the Islamic world, Africa and Oceania as well as Egyptian, Near Eastern and Mediterranean Antiquity. Visiting this gallery is like taking a voyage through time or passing through a gateway to the entire world. The images that have come down to us through the ages and from the four corners of the globe make use of unlimited combinations of style and form.

The objects that have successfully undergone this travel through time are seldom those meant for everyday use. The quality of the materials and the richness of the ornamentation bespeak a specific purpose, sacred ritual, representational roles or princely treasures. They have been preserved only because they were sheltered from the elements or kept in exceptionally favourable surroundings. But rather than reconstruct a temple or a sepulchre, the Museum has tried to create an environment that not only exposes the works to our view today, but also conserves them for tomorrow.

The place of origin of a three-thousand-year-old terra-cotta statuette is identified as Amlash, to the north of Iran's present-day borders.

The clearly defined sexual characteristics and the association of the human form with the animal form seen in this female figure tell of traditions that are even older than the statuette itself. With a prominent nose that might just as well be a beak, stumps for arms that resemble wings and the rounded body of a sitting hen, this bird-woman unmistakably evokes the image of fertility.

Roman emperor at the age of fourteen, Alexander Severus Marcus Aurelius (about 208-235) was killed twelve years later during a military expedition. He is remembered as a wise sovereign, open to the ideas of justice and tolerant of nascent Christianity. His portrait

shows the concern for realism and the characteristic simplification of the Empire's last centuries.

Although glass was invented in Ancient Egypt, the technique of glass blowing to create vessels dates from the Roman Empire. The Museum has a rich collection of Roman glass

**3**

According to sacred Buddhist tradition, the *Bodhisattva Maitreya* called the future Buddha, will come into the world to renew faith.

**4**

that was assembled by Harry A. Norton and his sister, Miss Helen Norton.

In this depiction, the Bodhisattva's cloth-ing, jewellery and hair style are those of a prince, while the "third eye" in the middle of the forehead, as well as the ornate halo with two praying figures, indicates his sacred character. A certain family resemblance with classical Greek statuary (in the pro-file and folds of the toga) recalls the links that the ancient kingdoms of the Silk Route maintained with the Mediter-ranean world.

The many commemorative heads,

each molded in the memory of a deceased *oba* (king) of the ancient kingdom of Benin (present-day Nigeria), by his successor, are more on the order of generalized representations than portraits. Crowned with a carved ivory tusk, these heads were designed to be displayed on a long sheltered altar that consisted of a roofed-over platform inside the court of royal palaces.

Chinese painting is inextricably linked with calligraphy: they both employ the same bold brush stroke, the same expressive use of line to attain an aesthetic and poetic ideal. Landscapes, seen in full view or in detail, express better than anything else the unity and the beauty of nature.

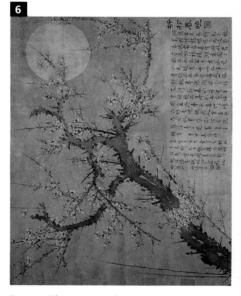

*Prunus Blossoms and Moon* is by Tong Yu (1721-1782), a poet and sculptor who collected antique bronze seals.

Nature inspires the choice of subject for the *kogo*,

**7**

or incense box. Each of these boxes, with their infinite variety of colours and motifs, reveals the special interest the Japanese show for life in all its forms. This chubby figure, or "Ofuka", a good luck charm, is but one of the some two thousand pieces bequeathed to the Museum by the Simard family.

This large brass hemispherical bowl, the first Islamic work to enter the Museum's collection, was originally engraved and inlaid with silver.

**8**

It was executed towards the middle of the 13th century for a sultan of Aleppo and Damascus, in Syria.

# The Americas
## Benaiah Gibb Pavilion
### (1912, 1939 and 1976)

The Benaiah Gibb Pavilion, on the north side of Sherbrooke Street, is devoted to art of the Americas: Canadian art before 1960, Meso-American art, Inuit art and Amerindian art. This section of the Museum also includes galleries for temporary exhibitions, educational areas, and the Prints and Drawings Galleries.

Over a thousand years ago, artists in Mexico and Central America produced extraordinary terra-cotta figurines,

**9**

each with its own unique facial features and expressive pose. This figurine depicts a *Seated Old Man* wearing a wry smile. He is perhaps the Old Fire God.

Some forty Inuit hunters marooned on a drifting ice floe escaped by hastily building a little boat with seal pelts. Sculptor Joe Talirunili was a child when he lived through this ordeal, but his stone sculpture has fixed forever in time the anguish of this *Migration*.

**10**

Towards the end of the 18th century, a number of talented artists and artisans went to Europe to complete their apprenticeship.

**11**

It was there that goldsmith Laurent Amiot acquired, in addition to his technical knowledge, the habit of working on his creations from drawings. He satisfied all his clients' requirements, whether for religious objects or domestic utensils, place settings and tea services for the bourgeoisie, like this sober *Teapot*.

15

which dates from the late 18th century, shows with what great skill Canadian artisans adapted the forms and motifs created in France during the reign of Louis XV to furniture for everyday use. With its ornamentation of fruit—a symbol of plenty—and baskets decorated with hearts, this buffet was without doubt the crowning glory of a bride's bountiful trousseau.

At one time, as soon as the village steeple faded from sight, crosses, placed where roads intersected, dotted the Quebec countryside. It was during the late 19th century that Pierre Plante, a farmer with great skill in fashioning familiar images from pine, executed this *Calvary*.

**13**

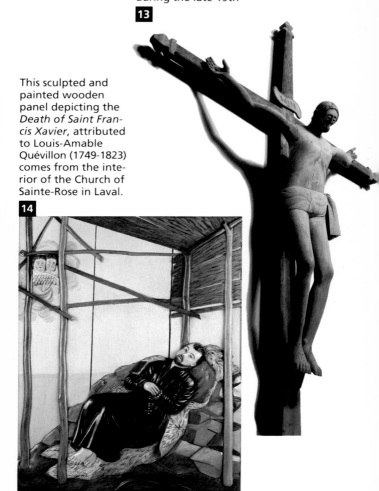

This sculpted and painted wooden panel depicting the *Death of Saint Francis Xavier*, attributed to Louis-Amable Quévillon (1749-1823) comes from the interior of the Church of Sainte-Rose in Laval.

**14**

The subject, treated countless times by painters and sculptors, recalls the popularity in Quebec – long the domain of Jesuit missionaries – of the cult of Saint Francis Xavier.

17

The representation of nature in New France did not really begin until the arrival of British landscape artists, the majority of whom were military topographers. For Joseph Légaré, who drew inspiration from works by these

**15**

artists, his canvas *Quebec City Seen from Pointe Lévis* is more than a picturesque scene: it demonstrates that he has taken hold of his ancestral country through painting.

Paul Kane had always been fascinated by the Plains Indians. This artist of Irish origin accompanied the Indians on their nomadic wanderings for months on end.

**16**

The some five hundred drawings that he brought back from excursions such as these served as sketches for paintings like *Caw-Wacham*, a depiction of the so-called Flat Head Indians that is at once classical in its pictorial treatment and documentary in content.

The still lifes of Ozias Leduc, despite the apparent simplicity of their subjects, are stirring, enigmatic works of a genuinely symbolic kind. The *Still Life with Open Book*,

which by including a violin and bow as well as a detail of the *Madonna of the Rosary* by Botticelli, pays tribute to pictorial art, music and knowledge.

James Wilson Morrice, the most exotic of the Montreal painters, spent a great deal of his life tracking down the brilliance of a summer afternoon or the rosy glow of a sunset beneath the skies of Brittany, Venice, North Africa and the West Indies.

**18**

As in *Venice, Looking Out over the Lagoon*, the subject is never more than a pretext for highlighting shapes or contrasting colours.

In Quebec during the first half of the 20th century, the majority of artists and writers drew inspiration from traditional rural life. However, Adrien Hébert was one of the first artists to opt for modern subjects. He saw as much poetry and grandeur in streets and public squares as in classical subjects.

**19**

In *Montreal Harbour*, he invites us "to lend an ear to the music of the mechanical sounds and the screams and wails of the siren".

Painter and sculptor Marc-Aurèle de Foy Suzor-Coté belonged to a generation of artists who, since the early 20th century, have tried to reconcile new art trends with classical tradition.

**20**

The allegory, which gives human form to abstract ideas, holds an important place in Alfred Laliberté's art.

**21**

*Caughnawaga Women* depicts a moment in time: the impression of fleeting shadows that pass in a muffled rustling.

To give substance to his conception of art and beauty, he chose the renowned statue *Venus de Milo* as his inspiration for *Déesse* [The Goddess], which was exhibited at the Art Association of Montreal in 1923.

The name of Jean-Marie Gauvreau is indissociable from the founding of the École du Meuble (1935) and the introduction of Art Deco to Montreal.

**22**

A *Dressing Table* (with pouf) is among the first pieces of furniture designed by Gauvreau during his studies at the École Boulle in Paris between 1928 and 1930.

A student of Ozias Leduc and later a teacher at the École du Meuble de Montréal, Paul-Émile Borduas is identified in particular with artistic and intellectual movements of the early 1940s that signalled the end of a conservative, rural Quebec.

**23**

His art culminated in *The Black Star*, from which figurative representation is totally absent and the use of colour is reduced to black and white.

Like his companion Borduas, Riopelle is identified with Automatism, or spontaneous painting, which is free of purpose and preconceived ideas. Riopelle had been in Paris for some years when he painted *Austria*.

**24**

By working with a palette knife loaded with paint, which he spread liberally on the canvas, he achieved a heavy impasto with the effects of iridescent enamel.

Far from being put off by the prevalence of abstract art, artists like Alex Colville turned to the observation of nature with renewed vigour.

**25**

A seemingly frozen immobility that roots people and things to the spot, as in *Church and Horse*, gives an air of mystery that goes far beyond the reality of the subjects depicted, whence the frequent use of the term "magic realism" to describe Colville's art.

The commotion caused in its time by Robert Roussil's *The Family* may perhaps have made people lose sight of the monumental force of this composition. This work created from a tree is a perfect example of one of the great constants in modern sculpture: the identification of form with medium.

Of all the Cana-
dians who lived in
Paris during the
first half of this
century, Alfred
Pellan is one of the
first to be touched
by the strong cur-
rents of Cubism and
Surrealism.

**27**

*L'amour fou* [Mad
Love], an homage to
André Breton, high
priest of Surrealism,
is a quest for beauty,
desire and the abso-
lute.

## Prints and Drawings

Caricature, like comedy, is the magnifying mirror through which we view the failings of society. More than mere illustrations of current events, Honoré Daumier's caricatures convey a truth and an expressive force that make them universal art. Nowhere is this more obvious than in The *Critics*, or *Visitors in a Painter's Studio*.

The precision and power of drawing associated with a concern for the minutest realistic detail better served Albrecht Dürer the printmaker than Albrecht Dürer the painter.

**29**

In the spirit of the Renaissance, his treatment of the *Adam and Eve* theme recalls that men and women, although banished from earthly Paradise, remain the lords of creation.

## Occidental Art, Yesterday and Today
Jean-Noël Desmarais Pavilion (1991)

The new pavilion, located at the south side of the underground gallery, contains a permanent display of European paintings, sculptures and decorative arts from the Middle Ages to the 19th century, and contemporary international and Canadian art executed after 1960.

The best examples of non-sculptural medieval art are tapestries, frescoes and stained glass.

**30**

Stained glass, associated with the decoration of Gothic churches, fulfils a narrative function by presenting episodes from Scripture or the lives of saints, as seen in this fragment *Joachim's Offering in the Temple*. The symbolic power of light and the transparency of stained glass lend this medium a spiritual dimension.

In the 16th century, sculptors and architects gained inspiration from ancient monuments – sources that painters did not have the equivalent of until the 18th century, when the first of Pompeii's frescoes were discovered. Some, like Mantegna, endeavoured through drawing and shading techniques to create the illusion of sculpture in relief. The subject borrowed from Roman legend is *Dido*, the amorous queen who, abandoned by Prince Aeneas, immolated herself on a funeral pyre.

**31**

In the 16th century, sacred figures were often depicted on the same plane as ordinary mortals, as in *Mary and Christ Interceding for Mankind* by Gherardo di Giovanni. The only distinguishing features are relative proportion and clothing.

The bird's-eye-view landscape in the background tells of the importance of the cities and urban activity.

**32**

Nicolas Poussin is known as the most Italian of the French artists because of his lengthy stay in Rome and his references to classical literature.

**33**

*Landscape with a Man Pursued by a Snake* depicts an ancient legend in which the inhabitants of Campania, disciples of Pythagoras, refused to kill the snakes infesting their region because they believed this animal to be sacred.

*Apelles Painting the Portrait of Campaspe* is what may be called a "painting within a painting".

**34**

Using history as pretext, Tiepolo reconstituted his own studio and depicted himself as the painter Apelles. He chose his wife Cecilia Guardi (sister of the painter Francesco Guardi) as his model for Campaspe. Tiepolo's depiction of Alexander the Great granting Apelles his true love, Campaspe, acknowledges the importance of the artist in society.

With the development of trade with the East, Europeans discovered a new type of fine, translucent porcelain, which they were eager to reproduce. When at last they discovered the secret, their success was so great that in the early 19th century, manufacturers could barely keep up with the demand. The Pair of Vases with polychrome and gold decoration come from factories in Derby founded in the middle of the 18th century.

**35**

The vases belong to the Lucile Pillow collection of English porcelain (1745-1840).

The 18th century in England was an era of great land holders with sumptuous country estates surrounded by parks and gardens. For portrait artists of the gentry, the portrayal of a person became almost inseparable from a landscape depiction of the person's estate. This *Portrait of Mrs. George Drummond*

by Thomas Gainsborough shows Martha, eldest daughter of Alderman Thomas Harley, at the time of her marriage in 1779.

The two Sablet brothers worked together so well that the work of one is often mistaken for that of the other. Jacques executed this *Portrait of a Family in front of*

*a Harbour.* The figures are outlined against a light-coloured background that is somewhat reminiscent of a theatre set or an antique frieze. This work is a perfect example of the paintings executed during the late 18th century, at which time the discovery of the ruins of Pompeii inspired artists to revert to the style and manner of Classical Rome.

Ludmille Komar and her sister Delphine, Countess Potocka, were actively involved in the intellectual and artistic life in Paris.

**38**

Forms and images drawn from Greco-Roman art recur time and time again.

**39**

In this portrait by Paul Delaroche, the delicacy of the work, the warm and brilliant colouring, and the luxuriousness of the fabric render the elegant and refined world to which *Ludmille Komar, Princess of Beauvau-Craon* belongs.

Beneath the apparent classical rigour of Jean-Jacques Pradier's *Standing Sappho*, we detect the mixture of romantic melancholy and repressed eroticism in which 19th-century artists often clothed the tragic loves of the Greek poetess.

Of the various, often contradictory, trends in vogue during the 19th century, the Royal Academy of Painting in France advocated the continuation of classical tradition.

While William Bouguereau ascribed to the tenets of Academism, he chose a pastoral subject for *Crown of Flowers*, rather than a mythological one. Although he re-

placed nymphs with peasants and shepherds, Bouguereau maintained his figures' air of affectionate seduction.

**40**

An autumn allegory, *October* is a tribute by James Tissot to Mrs. Newton, his beloved model.

**41**

This work is a fine example of a composition inspired from Japanese prints in which the figures in foreground stand out clearly against the contrasting background. The chestnut leaves that frame the composition and the horizon masked by a grouping of barely visible deer provide an ideal setting for the central figure.

The *Display of enchantment* is an imaginative work that is perhaps inspired from the opera *Tristan und Isolde* by Wagner.

In the 19th century, the "Orient" referred to the whole of the Mediterranean basin – from Moorish Spain to Byzantium– which bore the influence of the Islamic world. Poets and ar-

tists, following in the steps of Byron, Delacroix and Flaubert, drew inspiration from the exotic and at times colourful sensuality, as in *Evening on the Terrace in Morocco* by Jean-Joseph Benjamin Constant.

With this painting its creator, Henri Fantin-Latour, took part in the famous Salon des refusés in Paris in 1863, along with Manet, Pissaro, Cézanne and many others. It was this exhibition that marked the point of no return in the development of modern European painting.

Portraits of women
and girls, like *Young
Girl with Hat*,

**44**

frequently served
Pierre Auguste Renoir
as the pretext for
pictorial research in
which warm, earthy
colours and purple
shading vie with tex-
ture and impasto.
The finish of Renoir's
work is very differ-
ent from the porce-
lainized or over-
polished finishes of
Academic painting
in the style of
Bouguereau.

To the gamut of pastoral scenes preferred by the Impressionists are added scenes of train stations and factories, such as this *View of the Oissel Cotton Mill, near Rouen* by Camille Pissarro.

With their steely blue steam and their pink chimneys, these witnesses to the industrial revolution proclaim – every bit as much as artistic and political revolutions – the coming of a new age.

Georges Rouault
painted the seamy
side of circus, carni-
val and brothel life –
worlds generally
associated with
pleasure. His work
culminated with the
depiction of the
world of justice in
which judges and

**46**

the accused merge
in a common misery.
Set off with blue,
shaded with black,
compositions such as
*Christ Crucified*
recall the religious
intensity of medieval
stained glass.

American Lyonel Feininger, a member of the Bauhaus school, lived in pre-Hitler Germany during one of modern history's most crucial periods.

**47**

*Yellow Street II* is both Expressionist in its scale of colours and Cubist in its flattened and superimposed planes.

The art of sculptor Henry Spencer Moore respects his medium's form and texture and tends to resemble primitive art. For anatomical realism, Moore substituted a simplification that suggests ancient idols, and life and fertility symbols. It is tempting to thus compare *La Parze*

**48**

with the statuette from Amlash, shown on page 11.

It is said of Henri Matisse that he knew better than anyone else how to organize coloured sensations.

**49**

*Seated Woman, Back Turned to the Open Window* is but one of the many variations on the use of the window to bring together closed and open spaces. This theme is seen in works by Matisse and other painters.

Salvador Dalí
painted *Portrait of*

*Maria Carbona* in
his youth. At the
time, he had not yet
renounced Picasso's
influence, nor had
he begun to display
Surrealist motiva-
tion. Maria Carbona's
family were friends
of the Dalís and the
painting remained
in her possession
until the Museum
acquired it in 1969.

Alberto Giacometti,
in *Head of a Man on
Stele I*, calls into
question not only
sculpture's conventio-
nal forms, but also our
way of looking at the
world. By modifying
the proportional
relationship of his
subjects' height and
width and untiringly
reworking the planes
to streamline the
contours, he intro-
duces a feeling of
perspective.

Abstract art, born of experience with shapes and space, colour and texture, vacillated throughout this century between geometrical rigour and a freedom of movement that is translated by the play of impasto and dribblings.

**52**

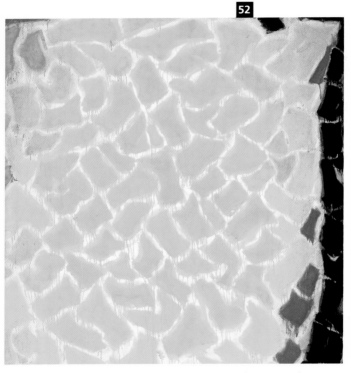

*Abstraction* by Sam Francis, an American painter working in Paris, belongs to the trend known as Lyrical Abstraction, which reached its peak after World War II.

Because the boundaries of "contemporary" and "traditional" are established according to stylistic rather than chronological criteria, we tend to forget that the Museum, and before it the Art Association of Montreal, began acquiring works by contemporary artists – that is artists still living – during the late 19th century. Today, the Museum's collection of "contemporary art" includes artists from Canada and abroad who produced work after 1960.

Present-day artists are pursuing the freedom of expression that began during the last century and are diversifying it even more – if that's possible! More than ever before, genres that previously could be neatly categorized are overstepping their boundaries to merge and mutually enhance each other. An almost life-size photographic enlargement, framed with wood and illuminated by a flame after the manner of certain early masters, *Door*, by Michael Snow, plays on our perception of depth, volume and relative proportion.

**53**

51

Leon Golub creates
huge works like
*Mercenaries II*

**54**

to compensate for
the effect the media
has of making all
forms of violence
appear routine. The
aggressors and
tormentors that he
depicts shock us only
if we forget to what
extent similar
themes – calvaries
and crucifixions –
have predominated
in Western art over
the centuries.

Contemporary artists
have a tendency to
replace standard
mythological and
literary subjects with
either representative
collective symbols or
elements from their
lives and their per-
sonal experiences.

**55**

Thus, *Back-Support
for a Fine-Limbed
Person (Hare-Type)
of the 20th Century
A.D.* by Joseph Beuys
belongs to a system
of individual sym-
bols to which he
alone holds the key.

*Sentiero* [Path]

**56**

by Giuseppe Penone is a single-cast bronze. In the manner of ancient or classical masters, Penone has used one of the sculptor's most noble mediums to display his personal interpretation of the close relationships that exist between man and nature.

Betty Goodwin's
mural *Carbon*,
**57**

peopled with black
and white figures,
examines the expres-
sive qualities of the
human body. This
theme, linked to the
body's fragility, runs
as a constant through
the artist's work.

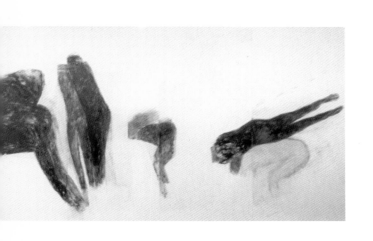

Mark Tansey questions both the notion of genre and historic times.

In *Action Painting II*, traditional easel painting, the work of Sunday-afternoon amateurs, photographs and collages blend in a monochromatic harmony that completely eliminates any impression of distance or depth. The subject suggested by the blast-off of a rocket brings us back to Jackson Pollock and American painting of the fifties and sixties.

by Montrealer Geneviève Cadieux plays on the inter-penetration of the senses suggested by the title of a poem written centuries ago by a Portuguese nun who was con-demned to silence for having proclaimed women's right to education. The pho-tographic installa-tion also reflects on the nature of media images, which are constantly being manipulated and cropped.

Like so many other sculptors, David Rabinowitch feels the need to organize space through drawing.

**60**

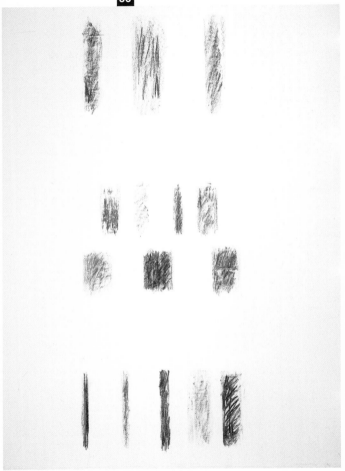

*Aposiopesis* belongs to the series with the revealing title "Construction of Vision". With an astonishing economy of means, he explores and exploits the possibilities of a sheet of white paper simply by varying shapes and the intensity of lines.

# List of illustrated works

## Let's start in the middle...

**1** Iran, *Steatopygous Female Figure*, terra-cotta, about 1200-1000 B.C., 47.5 x 18.7 cm, gift of David Y. Hodgson, 1963.Ea.1.

**2** Anonymous, *Emperor Severus Alexander*, marble, 3rd c., 28 x 12 x 12 cm, purchase, Horsley and Annie Townsend Bequest, 1968.1600.

**3** Flask, glass, 1st-2nd c., 13.3 x 2.5 x 6.4 cm, gift of Harry A. Norton, 1953.Dg.83a.

**4** Gandhāra, Kushān dynasty (50-320 A.D.), *Bodhisattva Maitreya*, grey schist, 3rd c., 118.1 cm (height), purchase, Horsley and Annie Townsend Bequest, 1976.Eb.1.

**5** Nigeria, Benin, *Commemorative Head*, bronze, 19th c., 47 cm (height), 30.5 x 33 cm (base), gift of F. Cleveland Morgan, 1950.51.F.5.

**6** Tong Yu, *Prunus Blossoms and Moon*, 1764, ink on silk, 74.3 x 94 cm, gift of A.W. Bahr, Dr.1986(946.Ed.9).55.

**7** Minpei-Yaki, Japan, *Kogo, Lady*, porcelain with polychrome enamel decoration, about 1830, 6.5 cm, gift of Joseph-Arthur Simard, 1960.Ee.500.

**8** Syria, Ayyubid (1176-1250), Bowl, brass, engraved and originally inlaid with silver, about 1250, 52 cm (diameter), gift of F. Cleveland Morgan, 1917.Ea.1.

## The Americas

**9** Mexico, Early classic (250-550 A.D.), *Seated Old Man*, pottery, 34 cm (height), purchase, Horsley and Annie Townsend Bequest, 1975.Ac.5.

**10** Joe Talirunili, *The Migration*, stone, bone, skin, 1965, 32.8 x 18.2 x 29.5 cm, gift of John G. McConnell, 1974.Aa.2.

**11** Laurent Amiot, Teapot, silver and wood, about 1805, 15.1 x 28.4 cm, Ramsay Traquair Bequest, 1952.Ds.41.

**12** Quebec, Two-tiered Buffet, pine, 1775-1799, 255 x 155 x 65.1 cm, gift of Miss Mabel Molson, 1938.Df.13.

**13** Pierre Plante, *Calvary*, pine, 1888, 426.6 cm, purchase, Horsley and Annie Townsend Bequest, 1965.Df.1.

**14** Louis-Amable Quévillon, *Death of Saint Francis Xavier*, about 1811-1816, painted and carved wood, 93.5 x 74.8 cm, gift of Samuel Breitman, 1964.Df.17.

**15** Joseph Légaré, *View of Quebec City from Pointe-Lévis*, 1842-1843, oil on canvas, 90 x 120 cm, gift of the J.A. DeSève Estate and Horsley and Annie Townsend Bequest, 1980.3.

**16** Paul Kane, *Caw-Wacham*, 1845-1848, oil on canvas, 76.2 x 63.4 cm, purchase, Gilman Cheney Bequest, 1947.991.

**17** Ozias Leduc, *Still Life with Open Book*, 1894, oil on canvas, 38.5 x 48 cm, purchase, gift of the Canadian Cultural Property Export Review Board, the Museum Volunteer Committee, 1985.7.

**18** James Wilson Morrice, *Venice, Looking Out Over the Lagoon*, about 1902-1904, oil on canvas, 60.6 x 73.9 cm, gift of the artist's estate, 1925.334.

**19** Adrien Hébert, *Montreal Harbour*, 1925, oil on canvas, 101.6 x 81 cm, purchase, Maurice Corbeil and Nahum Gelber Funds, 1985.6.

**20** Marc-Aurèle de Foy Suzor-Côté, *Caughnawaga Women*, bronze, 1924, 43.5 cm (height), gift of Mr. F.N. Southam, 1927.473.

**21** Alfred Laliberté, *Déesse* [Goddess], plaster, about 1923, 184 x 52 x 47 cm, purchase, Hugh G. Jones and Arthur Lismer funds, 1988.34.

**22** Jean-Marie Gauvreau, Pouf, ebony, amboyna and upholstery, about 1928-1930, 33 x 43 cm, purchase, Horsley and Annie Townsend Bequest, 1981.Df.5.5. Jean-Marie Gauvreau, Dressing Table, ebony and amboyna, about 1928-1930, 115 x 149 x 38 cm, purchase, Horsley and Annie Townsend Bequest, 1981.Df.5.7.

**23** Paul-Émile Borduas, *The Black Star*, 1957, oil on canvas, 162.5 x 129.5 cm, gift of Mr. and Mrs. Gérard Lortie, 1960.1238.

**24** Jean-Paul Riopelle, *Austria*, 1954, oil on canvas, 200 x 300.7 cm, purchase, Horsley and Annie Townsend Bequest, 1963.1395.

**25** Alex Colville, *Church and Horse*, 1964, acrylic on masonite, 55.5 x 68.7 cm, purchase, Horsley and Annie Townsend Bequest and anonymous donor, 1966.1529.

**26** Robert Roussil, *The Family*, spruce, 1949, 318 x 74 x 66 cm, gift of Mr. Bernard Janelle, 1990.37.

**27** Alfred Pellan, *L'amour fou* [Mad Love], 1954, oil on canvas, 140.5 x 106 cm, purchase, Horsley and Annie Townsend Bequest, 1991.9.

Prints and Drawings

**28** Honoré Daumier, *The Critics (Visitors in a Painter's Studio)*, about 1862, pen and black ink, Conté crayon, watercolour and gouache, 36 X 45.1 cm, bequest of Mrs. William R. Miller in memory of her husband, 1951.1045.

**29** Albrecht Dürer, *Adam and Eve (The Fall of Man)*, 1504, engraving, 4th state of 5, 24.9 X 19.2 cm, purchase, Miss Olive Hosmer Fund, Gr.1961.81.

## Occidental Art, Yesterday and Today

**30** France, Gothic, *Joachim's Offering in the Temple*, stained glass (fragment), Abbey Church of Saint Germain-des-Prés, Lady Chapel, about 1245-1250, 63.5 x 90.2 cm, purchase, 1929.Dg.4.

**31** Andrea Mantegna, *Dido*, about 1500, tempera on linen, 65.3 x 31.4 cm, purchase, John W. Tempest Fund, 1920.104.

**32** Gherardo di Giovanni, *Christ and Virgin Interceding for Mankind*, about 1490, oil and tempera on panel, 87.6 x 55.2 cm, purchase, John W. Tempest Bequest, 1953.1084.

**33** Nicolas Poussin, *Landscape with a Man Pursued by a Snake*, about 1638-1639, oil on canvas, 65 x 76 cm, purchase, Special Replacement Fund, 1975.15.

**34** Giovanni Battista Tiepolo, *Apelles Painting the Portrait of Campaspe*, about 1725-1726, oil on canvas, 57.4 x 73.7 cm, Adaline Van Horne Bequest, 1945.929.

**35** England, Pair of Vases, Bloor Derby, porcelain, bone ash added, with overglaze painted decoration, in polychrome and gold, 1820, 33.95 x 27.94 cm, The Lucile E. Pillow Collection, 1964.Lp.185,186.

**36** Thomas Gainsborough, *Portrait of Mrs. George Drummond*, about 1779, oil on canvas, 230.1 x 152 cm, purchase, John W. Tempest Bequest, 1951.1062.

**37** Jacques Sablet the Younger, *Family Portrait in front of a Harbour*, 1800, oil on canvas, 65 x 81 cm, purchase, Special Replacement Fund, 1975.16.

**38** Hippolyte (called Paul) Delaroche, *Ludmille Komar, Princess of Beauvau-Craon*, 1849, oil on canvas, 71 x 58 cm, purchase, funds bequeathed by Dr. and Mrs. Max Stern, 1990.24.

**39** Jean-Jacques (called James) Pradier, *Standing Sappho*, silvered bronze, after 1848, 44.7 cm, purchase, Horsley and Annie Townsend Bequest, 1985.1.

**40** William Bouguereau, *Crown of Flowers*, 1884, oil on canvas, 162.9 x 89.9 cm, Gift of R.B. Angus, 1889.17.

**41** Jean-Jacques (called James) Tissot, *October*, 1877, oil on canvas, 216 x 108.7 cm, gift of Lord Strathcona and family, 1927.410.

**42** Henri Fantin-Latour, *Display of Enchantment*, 1863, oil on canvas, 98.8 x 131.5 cm, John W. Tempest Bequest, 1936.658.

**43** Jean-Joseph Benjamin Constant, called Benjamin-Constant, *Evening on the Terrace, Souvenir of Morocco*, 1879, oil on canvas, 123 x 198.5 cm, gift of Lord Strathcona and Family, 1927.243.

**44** Pierre Auguste Renoir, *Young Girl with a Hat*, about 1890, oil on canvas, 41.5 x 32.5 cm, purchase, contribution of the Government of Canada under the terms of the Cultural Property Export and Import Act, and gifts of Mrs. A.T. Henderson, the families of the late M. Dorothea Millar and the late J. Lesley Ross, the Bank of Montreal, Redpath Industries Ltd. and the Royal Trust Company, in memory of Huntly Redpath Drummond, 1984.17.

**45** Camille Pissarro, *View of the Cotton Mill at Oissel, near Rouen*, 1898, oil on canvas, 65.4 x 81 cm, purchase, John W. Tempest Fund, 1921.145.

**46** Georges Rouault, *Christ Crucified*, about 1939, oil on canvas, 76.9 x 59.5 cm, purchase, John W. Tempest Bequest, 1953.1088.

**47** Lyonel Feininger, *Yellow Street II*, 1918, oil on canvas, 95 x 86.1 cm, The Maxwell Cummings Family Foundation; The Ladies' Committee of the Museum; John G. McConnell, C.B.E., Mr. & Mrs. Murray A. Vaughan, Harold Lawson Bequest, Horsley and Annie Townsend Bequest, 1971.35.

**48** Henry Spencer Moore, *La Parze*, bronze, green patina, edition of 8, 1957-1958, 152.5 cm (height), gift of Dr. and Mrs. Max Stern, 1977.43.

**49** Henri Matisse, *Seated Woman, Back Turned to the Open Window*, 1922, oil on canvas, 73 x 92 cm, purchase, John W. Tempest Fund, 1949.1015.

**50** Salvador Dalí, *Portrait of Maria Carbona*, 1925, oil on wood, 53 x 39.7 cm, gift of the Ladies' Committee of the Museum, 1969.1640.

**51** Alberto Giacometti, *Head of a Man on Stele I*, bronze, 5/6, 1958, 161.3 cm (height), purchase, Horsley and Annie Townsend Bequest and gift of Mr. Charles Bronfman and Phyllis Lambert, Nahum Gelber, Q.C., Mr. H.G. Hallward, Mr. and Mrs. Peter Laing, Mr. and Mrs. Bernard Lamarre, Mr. Guy de Repentigny, Mr. and Mrs. Gershon Stern, the W.P. Scott Charitable Foundation, and anonymous donors, 1982.2.

**52** Sam Francis, *Abstraction*, 1954, oil on canvas, 197.7 x 185.8 cm, gift of Mr. and Mrs. Maurice Corbeil and Mr. Gilles Corbeil, 1961.1315.

Contemporary Art from Canada and Abroad

**53** Michael Snow, *Door*, 1979, photographic montage,
208.6 x 99.9 cm, purchase, Canada Council Matching Grant,
1979.32.

**54** Leon Golub, *Mercenaries II*, 1979, acrylic on canvas,
305 x 366 cm, purchase, Horsley and Annie Townsend
Bequest, 1983.1.

**55** Joseph Beuys, *Backrest for a Fine-Limbed Person (Hare-Type)
of the 20th Century A.D.*, cast iron, Seriaal Edition,
Amsterdam, 12/12, 1972, 96 x 45 x 15 cm, gift of Marielle and
Paul Mailhot, 1983.6.

**56** Giuseppe Penone, *Sentiero* [Path], bronze, single cast, 1983,
180 x 400 x 45 cm, purchase, Horsley and Annie Townsend
Bequest, 1983.36.

**57** Betty Goodwin, *Carbon*, 1986, charcoal powder, wax, oil
stick, pastel, graphite, oil and gesso on honeycomb galva-
nized aluminum, 275 x 975.6 cm, purchase, Horsley and Annie
Townsend Bequest, 1987.13a-h.

**58** Mark Tansey, *Action Painting II*, 1984, oil on canvas, 193 x
279.4 cm, gift of Mr. Nahum Gelber, Q.C, 1984.18.

**59** Geneviève Cadieux, *Hear Me with Your Eyes*, 1989, photographic installation: Cibachrome colour prints, silver gelatin
prints mounted on wooden screens, 3 elements measuring
244.8 x 305.3 cm each, 1989.40a,b,c.

**60** David Rabinowitch, *Aposiopesis* from the Series "Construction of Vision", 1982, Charcoal and beeswax on rag paper,
287 X 203.4 cm, purchase, The Saidye and Samuel Bronfman
Collection of Canadian Art, Dr.1984.125.

## General information

Telephone: (514) 285-1600

**Main Entrance and Ticket Counter**
1379-1380 Sherbrooke Street West

**Group Entrance**
2200 Crescent Street

**Services**
Carrefour
Boutique
Bookstore
Library
Slide Library
Art Sales and Rental Gallery
Cafeteria
Restaurant
Members' Lounge
Auditorium

**Access**
Bus 24 or Guy-Concordia metro

**Postal address:**
The Montreal Museum of Fine Arts
P.O. Box 3000, Station "H"
Montreal, Quebec
H3G 2T9